NATIONAL GEOGRAPHIC

Our World

This atlas belongs to

_____

NATIONAL GEOGRAPHIC SOCIETY
WASHINGTON, D.C.

Our World

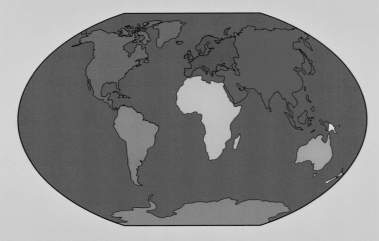

Editor's Note: This atlas will introduce very young children to the most basic concepts of geography: the seven continents, the four oceans that border them, and the countries located on them. With the help of our world-famous cartographers, the simplified maps have been designed to resemble giant puzzle pieces—boldly colored and easy to read. Children will be able to find most of the world's countries on them. Only the very smallest countries have been omitted to keep the maps uncluttered and readable.

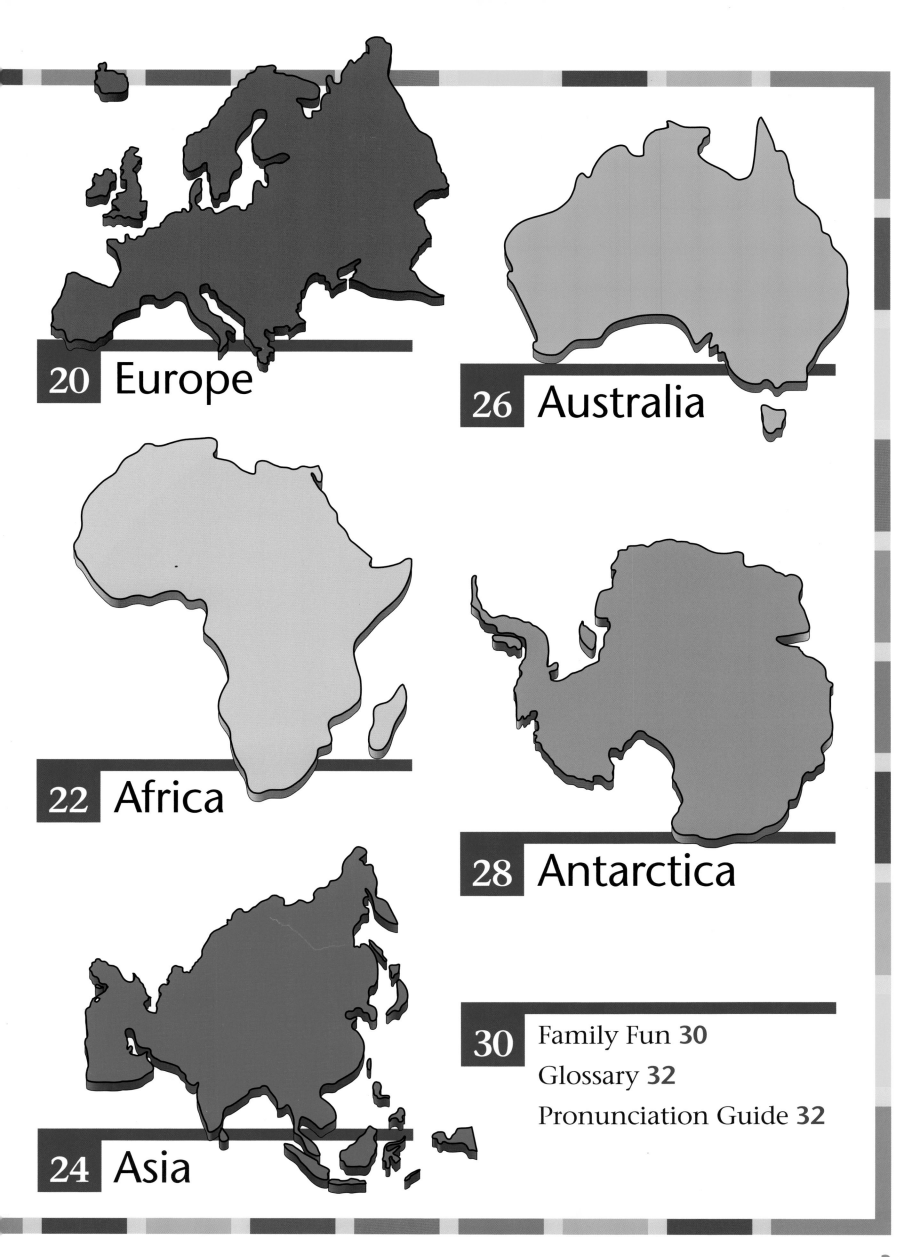

Earth to Globe

When astonauts take a rocket up into space, they see that planet Earth is really an enormous round ball. A globe is a small, round model of Earth. On a globe you see the planet as the astronauts do—one side at a time.

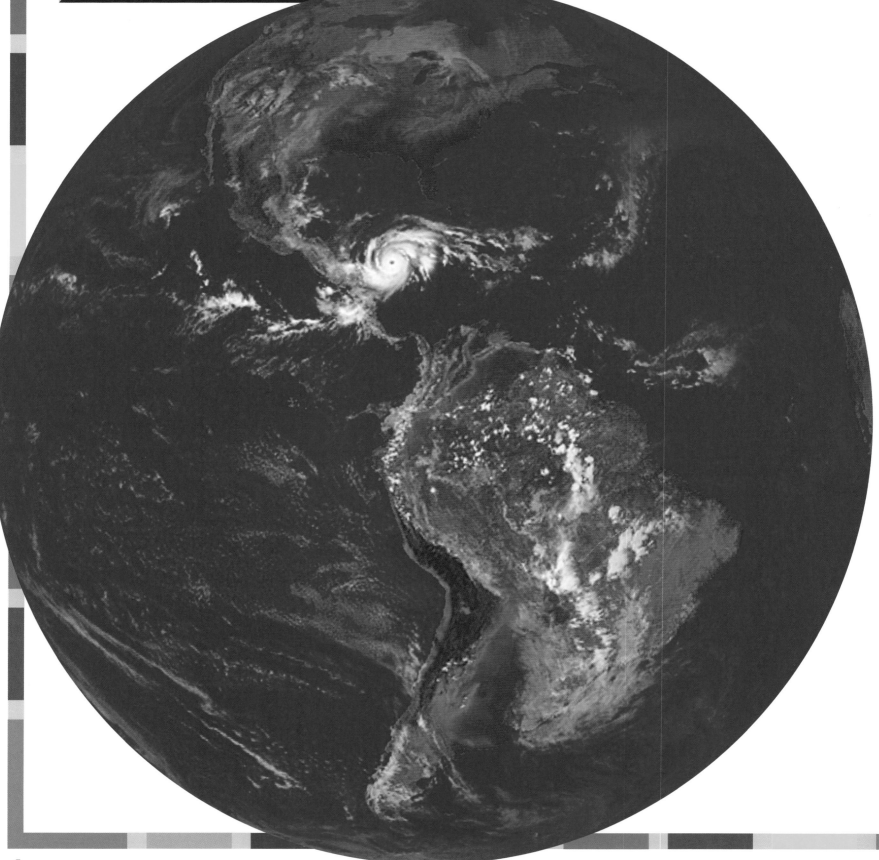

To see what's on the
other side of a **globe,**
all you have to do
is turn it.

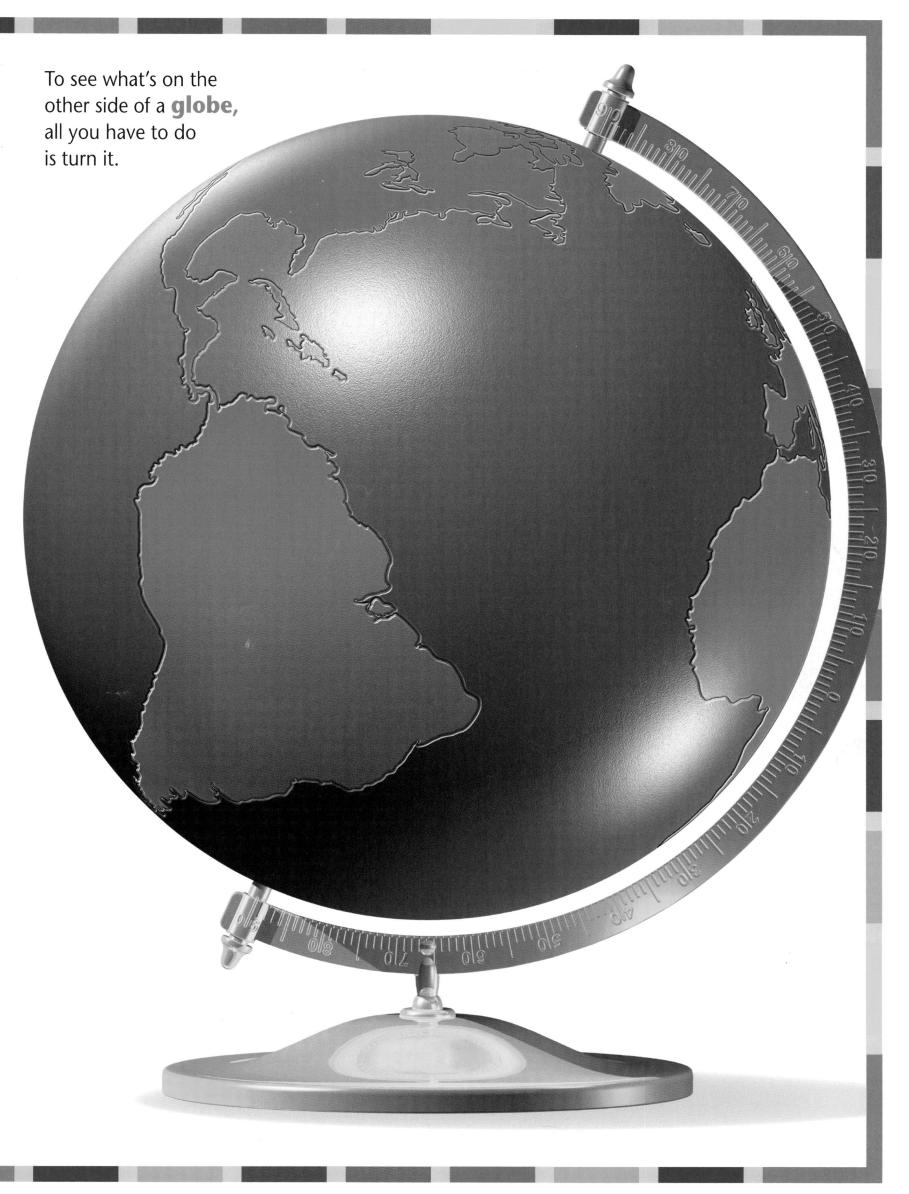

Earth as a Map

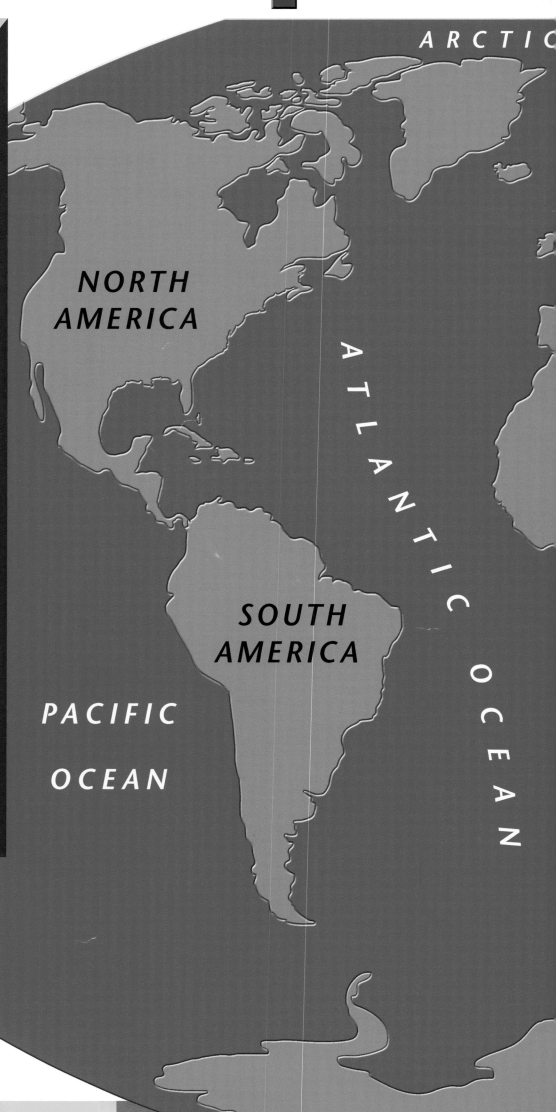

A map is a flat drawing of the Earth. It lets you see the whole Earth at one time. This map shows water in blue and land in green. The biggest pieces of land are called continents. The largest bodies of water are called oceans.

A compass like the one below shows directions on a map. For all the maps in this atlas, north (N) is at the top of the page, south (S) is at the bottom, east (E) is at the right edge of the page, and west (W) is at the left edge.

W

N
W   E
S

ARCTIC

NORTH AMERICA

ATLANTIC OCEAN

SOUTH AMERICA

PACIFIC OCEAN

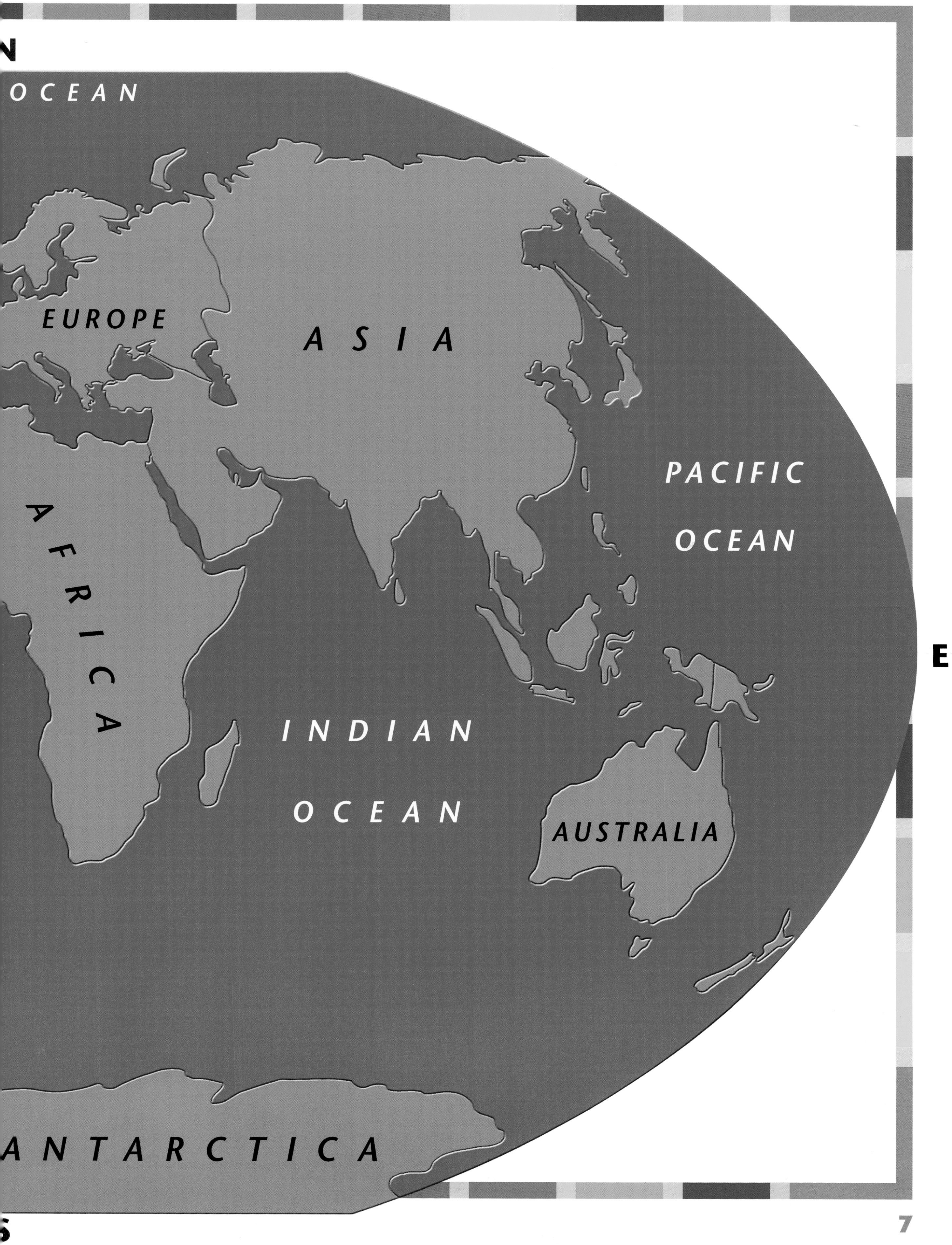

OCEAN

EUROPE

A S I A

A F R I C A

PACIFIC

OCEAN

I N D I A N

OCEAN

AUSTRALIA

A N T A R C T I C A

Looking at the Land

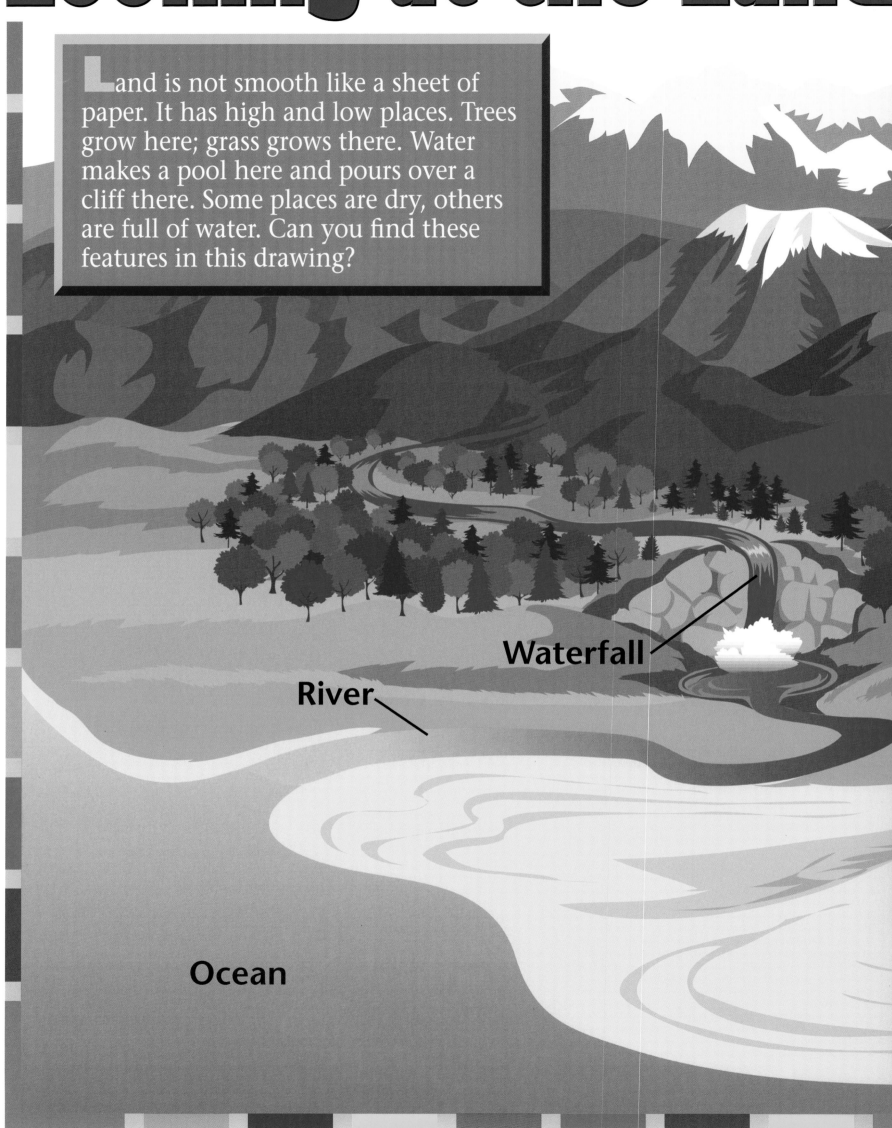

Land is not smooth like a sheet of paper. It has high and low places. Trees grow here; grass grows there. Water makes a pool here and pours over a cliff there. Some places are dry, others are full of water. Can you find these features in this drawing?

Waterfall

River

Ocean

Mountains

Volcano

Lake

Forest

Grassland

Desert

Land and Water

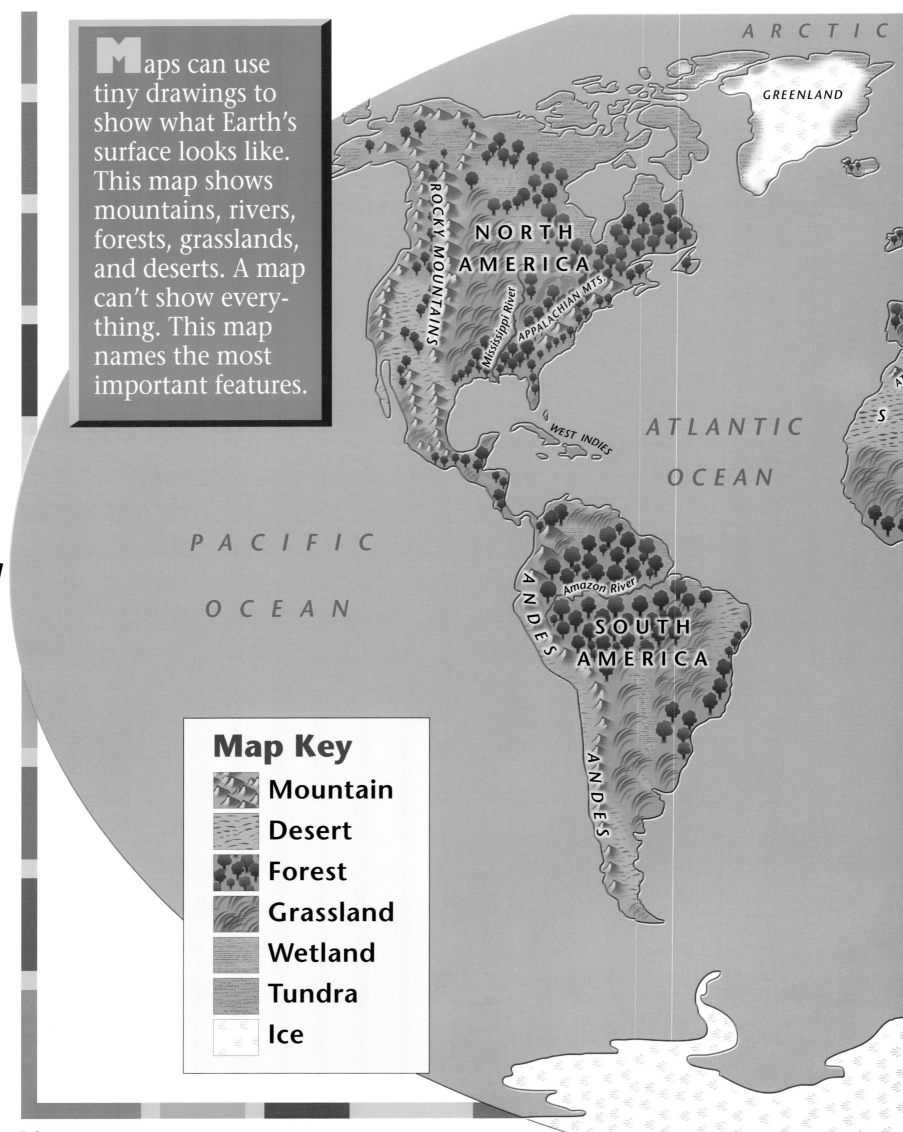

Maps can use tiny drawings to show what Earth's surface looks like. This map shows mountains, rivers, forests, grasslands, and deserts. A map can't show everything. This map names the most important features.

ARCTIC

GREENLAND

ROCKY MOUNTAINS

NORTH AMERICA

Mississippi River

APPALACHIAN MTS.

AT

S

ATLANTIC

OCEAN

WEST INDIES

PACIFIC

OCEAN

ANDES

Amazon River

SOUTH AMERICA

ANDES

Map Key

Mountain

Desert

Forest

Grassland

Wetland

Tundra

Ice

W

OCEAN

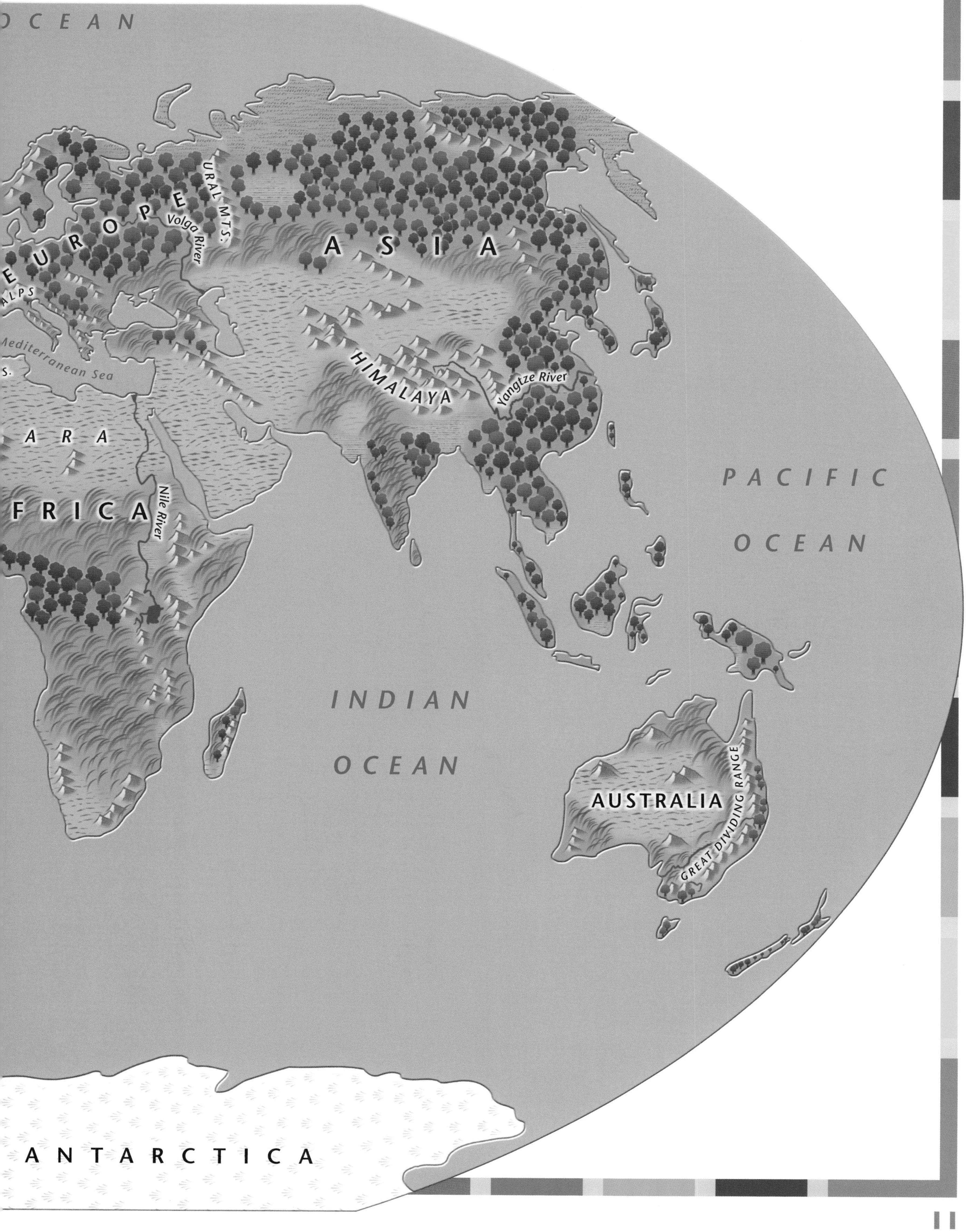

EUROPE

URAL MTS.

Volga River

ALPS

Mediterranean Sea

S.

A S I A

A R A

FRICA

Nile River

HIMALAYA

Yangtze River

PACIFIC

OCEAN

INDIAN

OCEAN

AUSTRALIA

GREAT DIVIDING RANGE

ANTARCTICA

Where People Live

W

People live in many countries around the world. This map shows countries in different colors so it's easy to see where one country ends and another begins. This map names many but not all of the countries in the world.

GREENLAND

UNITED STATES

CANADA

ICELAND

UNITED KINGDOM

IRELAND

UNITED STATES

PORTUGAL

MOROCCO

MEXICO

WESTERN SAHARA

MAURITANIA

BAHAMAS

CUBA

HAITI

DOMINICAN REPUBLIC

JAMAICA

PUERTO RICO

BELIZE

HONDURAS

SENEGAL

GAMBIA

GUINEA-BISSAU

GUINEA

GUATEMALA

EL SALVADOR

NICARAGUA

COSTA RICA

PANAMA

VENEZUELA

GUYANA

SURINAME

FRENCH GUIANA

SIERRA LEONE

LIBERIA

CÔTE D'IVOIRE

COLOMBIA

ECUADOR

BRAZIL

PERU

BOLIVIA

PARAGUAY

CHILE

ARGENTINA

URUGUAY

United States

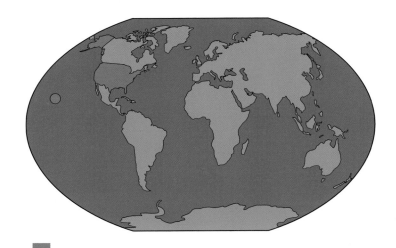

It's pumpkin-carving time! In the United States we hollow out pumpkins to make jack o' lanterns in autumn. The United States is on the continent of North America. People from all over the world live here. We call ourselves Americans.

◄ The **space shuttle** is a special rocket ship. The United States uses the shuttle to carry astronauts, scientists, and equipment into space and back.

Map note: To see the real locations of the states of Alaska and Hawaii, look at the small world map (top left).

Find These On the Map

There are many volcanoes in Hawaii and Alaska. Washington, Oregon, and California have some, too.

The Everglades is a huge swampy place in Florida. Alligators, birds, and lots of other animals live there.

▶ **Tornadoes** are powerful, funnel-shaped winds. They sometimes come with thunderstorms. The United States has more tornadoes than any other country in the world.

MONTANA

NORTH DAKOTA

MINNESOTA

MICHIGAN

WISCONSIN

NEW HAMPSHIRE

VERMONT

MAINE

IDAHO

SOUTH DAKOTA

NEW YORK

MASSACHUSETTS

WYOMING

IOWA

PENNSYLVANIA

RHODE ISLAND

CONNECTICUT

NEBRASKA

OHIO

NEW JERSEY

UTAH

COLORADO

ILLINOIS

INDIANA

WEST VIRGINIA

DELAWARE

MARYLAND

KANSAS

MISSOURI

KENTUCKY

VIRGINIA

ARIZONA

NEW MEXICO

OKLAHOMA

ARKANSAS

TENNESSEE

NORTH CAROLINA

SOUTH CAROLINA

TEXAS

LOUISIANA

MISSISSIPPI

ALABAMA

GEORGIA

FLORIDA

HAWAII

▶ The **Statue of Liberty** stands at the entrance to New York harbor. This symbol of freedom welcomes people to the United States.

The President of the United States lives in the White House. It is in Washington, D.C., the capital city.

Old Faithful is a spout of hot water. It shoots out of the ground in Yellowstone National Park.

North America

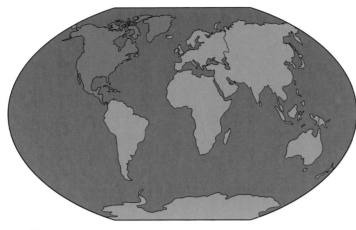

School is out! We live on one of the islands in the West Indies. These islands are part of North America. Greenland is, too. Our continent stretches from Canada all the way to Panama. Most people in North America speak English, Spanish, or French.

◀**Polar bears** live in the far north where there is ice and snow year-round. White fur helps them hide against the snow.

▼In North America farmers grow wheat, corn, and other crops. These farmers are **harvesting wheat** in Canada.

Find These On the Map

Mount McKinley is North America's highest mountain. It is also called Denali. Look for it in the northernmost U.S. state.

The Panama Canal is a waterway across Panama. Ships use it as a shortcut between the Atlantic and the Pacific Ocean.

GREENLAND

UNITED
STATES

C A N A D A

UNITED STATES

MEXICO

▼ There are many
cities along the
east coast of
North America.
New York is
the biggest.

BAHAMAS

CUBA

HAITI

DOMINICAN REPUBLIC

PUERTO
RICO

JAMAICA

BELIZE

GUATEMALA

HONDURAS

EL SALVADOR

NICARAGUA

COSTA RICA

PANAMA

The Mississippi River is
North America's biggest
river. This famous arch
stands along the river in
St. Louis, Missouri.

Huge stone faces
have been found
in Mexico. They
were carved by
people long ago.

South America

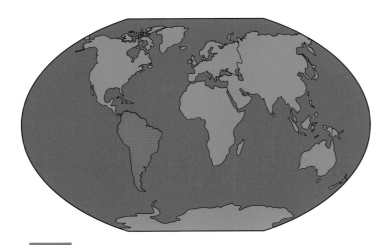

Fish for dinner, anyone? We caught this big fish in the Amazon River. I live in Brazil. It is the biggest country in South America. People in Brazil speak Portuguese. In almost every other country in South America people speak Spanish.

▼ Cowboys called **gauchos** herd cattle in grassy parts of Argentina and Uruguay. Beef is a popular food in South America.

Find These On the Map

Angel Falls is the highest waterfall in the world. To find it, you'd have to hike through the rain forest in Venezuela.

The Andes are high, snow-covered mountains. They stretch along the west coast from Colombia all the way to the tip of Chile.

VENEZUELA

COLOMBIA

GUYANA

SURINAME

FRENCH GUIANA

ECUADOR

PERU

BRAZIL

BOLIVIA

PARAGUAY

CHILE

ARGENTINA

URUGUAY

▶ Farmers in Ecuador ship **bananas** to markets all over the world.

▼Macaws are big, colorful birds. They live in the **rain forest** that grows along the Amazon River. Jaguars and monkeys live there, too.

▲Every year people celebrate **carnaval** in Brazil. They dress up in colorful costumes and parade through the streets.

Llamas are good at climbing mountains. People in the Andes use them to carry things. They also make warm blankets and ponchos from llama wool.

Some houses along the Amazon River stand on stilts. This huge river flows from Peru across Brazil to the Atlantic Ocean.

Europe

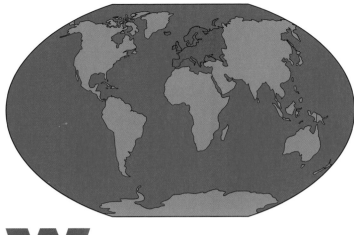

Would anyone like a pony ride? We live in Ireland, an island country in Europe. Europe has many long fingers of land called peninsulas that stick out into the sea. This means no place is very far from the water.

ICELA...

IRELAND

FRANC...

PORTUGAL

SPAIN

◄**Big Ben** is the bell in a famous clock tower in London. London is the capital city of the United Kingdom.

Find These On the Map

St. Basil's is the most famous church in Russia. The colorful rooftops are called onion domes because of their shape.

Iceland has more than 100 volcanoes and many hot springs. This island country also has many huge rivers of ice called glaciers.

Map note: The broken lines on the map mean the rest of these countries are in Asia. Look at the map on pages 24–25.

NORWAY

SWEDEN

FINLAND

ASIA

EUROPE

R U S S I A

ESTONIA

LATVIA

LITHUANIA

UNITED KINGDOM

DENMARK

NETHER-LANDS

RUSSIA

BELGIUM

GERMANY

POLAND

BELARUS

KAZAKHSTAN

LUXEMBOURG

CZECH REPUBLIC

U K R A I N E

SWITZERLAND

AUSTRIA

SLOVAKIA

HUNGARY

MOLDOVA

SLOVENIA

CROATIA

ROMANIA

AZERBAIJAN

ITALY

BOSNIA & HERZEGOVINA

YUGO-SLAVIA

BULGARIA

GEORGIA

MACEDONIA

TURKEY

ALBANIA

GREECE

◄ This woman is picking **grapes.** They are one of the many kinds of fruit that grow in southern Europe. Here, the weather is warm and sunny.

▲ Venice is a city in Italy. People there often travel along the city's canals in boats called **gondolas.**

Long ago, people in Greece believed gods and goddesses ruled the Earth. This god lived in a castle beneath the sea.

The Eiffel Tower is the most famous structure in Paris, France. For many years it was the tallest building in the world.

21

Africa

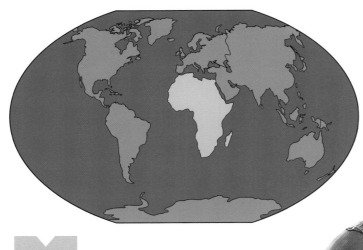

WESTERN
SAHARA

MAURITAN

SENEGAL

GAMBIA

GUINEA-
BISSAU

GUINEA

SIERRA LEONE

LIBERIA

Masai girls like to wear colorful bead-work. Our families herd cattle in East Africa. Most people in Africa are farmers or herders. Africa has more countries than any other continent. More than a thousand languages are spoken here.

▼ **Savannas** are grasslands that cover large areas in Africa. Herds of antelopes, zebras, elephants, and other animals graze here. Cheetahs come to hunt these animals for food.

▶ Only male **lions**, like this one, have a mane of hair around their heads. Lions live on Africa's grasslands in groups called prides.

Find These On the Map

Snow-capped Mount Kilimanjaro, in Tanzania, is the highest mountain in Africa.

In South Africa, miners dig for diamonds, gold, and other valuable materials. Mining is a dangerous job.

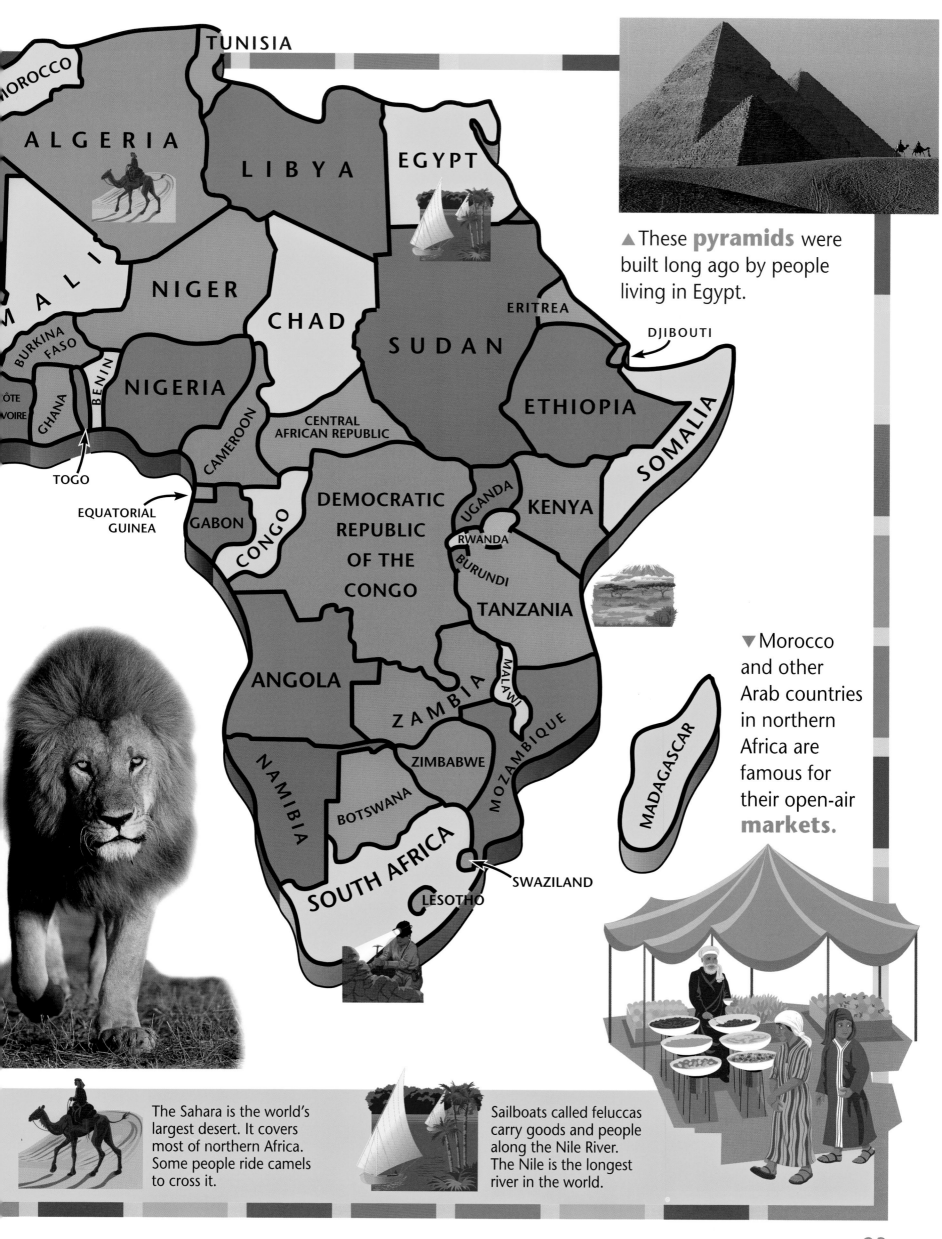

TUNISIA

MOROCCO

ALGERIA

LIBYA

EGYPT

▲ These **pyramids** were built long ago by people living in Egypt.

MALI

NIGER

CHAD

SUDAN

ERITREA

DJIBOUTI

BURKINA FASO

CÔTE D'IVOIRE

GHANA

BENIN

NIGERIA

CAMEROON

CENTRAL AFRICAN REPUBLIC

ETHIOPIA

SOMALIA

TOGO

EQUATORIAL GUINEA

GABON

CONGO

DEMOCRATIC REPUBLIC OF THE CONGO

UGANDA

RWANDA

BURUNDI

KENYA

TANZANIA

ANGOLA

ZAMBIA

MALAWI

▼ Morocco and other Arab countries in northern Africa are famous for their open-air **markets.**

NAMIBIA

ZIMBABWE

BOTSWANA

MOZAMBIQUE

MADAGASCAR

SOUTH AFRICA

SWAZILAND

LESOTHO

The Sahara is the world's largest desert. It covers most of northern Africa. Some people ride camels to cross it.

Sailboats called feluccas carry goods and people along the Nile River. The Nile is the longest river in the world.

Asia

Welcome to Asia! I live in a part of China called Tibet. More people live in China than in any other country in Asia. This continent has the most people, the most land, and the highest mountains.

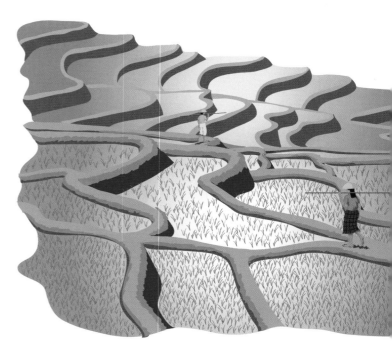

◄ Bamboo is the **panda's** favorite food. In the wild these animals live only in China in places where bamboo forests grow.

Find These On the Map

Mount Everest is the highest mountain in the world. It is almost six miles high!

The Great Wall of China was built hundreds of years ago to keep out enemies. It is about 3,000 miles long.

Map note: The broken lines on the map mean that the rest of these countries are in Europe. Look at the map on pages 20–21.

EUROPE

ASIA

RUSSIA

RBAIJAN

KAZAKHSTAN

UZBEKISTAN

KMENISTAN

KYRGYZSTAN

TAJIKISTAN

AFGHANISTAN

PAKISTAN

NEPAL

BHUTAN

INDIA

MONGOLIA

CHINA

NORTH KOREA

JAPAN

SOUTH KOREA

MYANMAR

LAOS

THAILAND

BANGLADESH

VIETNAM

CAMBODIA

SRI LANKA

PHILIPPINES

BRUNEI

MALAYSIA

INDONESIA

▼ Many people in India believe the **Ganges River** has the power to heal the sick. Millions of people live along its banks and bathe in it.

◄ Rice is the main food eaten in Asia. Farmers often grow it on steplike fields called **terraces.** These fields are cut into steep hillsides.

The city of Jerusalem is a religious center for Jews, Christians, and Muslims. Most of the world's major religions began in Asia.

Japan is a very high-tech country. Its fastest trains are called bullet trains. They carry millions of people to and from work each day.

Australia

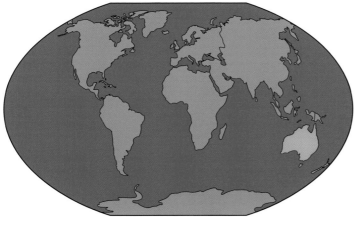

▲Australia has lots of **sheep.** Here, a rancher herds sheep into a pen.

Look, I've found a starfish! Australia's Great Barrier Reef is full of all kinds of sea life. Water is all around Australia, but the continent is mostly desert. Australia is the smallest continent. It is also the only one that has just one country—Australia!

▼Many roads in Australia are straight and flat. That's because most of Australia is **desert.** Drivers here have to be on the lookout for kangaroos!

Find These On the Map

The roof of the Sydney Opera House looks like sails on a boat. Sydney is Australia's largest city.

The Tasmanian devil raises its young in a pouch on its tummy. It is called "devil" because it makes screamlike noises.

AUSTRALIA

TASMANIA

◄ The cuddly-looking **koala** lives only in Australia. Koalas eat eucalyptus leaves. That's why they smell a bit like cough drops!

The Great Barrier Reef is the longest coral reef in the world. It lies beneath shallow ocean waters off Australia's east coast.

Ayers Rock rises from the desert in the middle of Australia. It is far from any large city. Tourists drive for hours to see it.

Antarctica

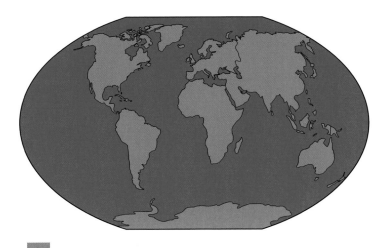

If you visited Antarctica, you would see penguins and seals, mountains and valleys, and snow and ice. The continent is so cold, people come only for visits, not to live. There aren't any cities, but you will find scientists at work. Antarctica is the only continent that has no countries.

◄ **Scientists** come to Antarctica from other continents. They stay for a few chilly weeks or months. These researchers are using a balloon to study the weather.

Find These On the Map

Antarctica has many mountains and even some volcanoes. Mount Erebus is the world's southernmost volcano.

The South Pole is the southernmost point on the Earth. It is marked by flags and a pole.

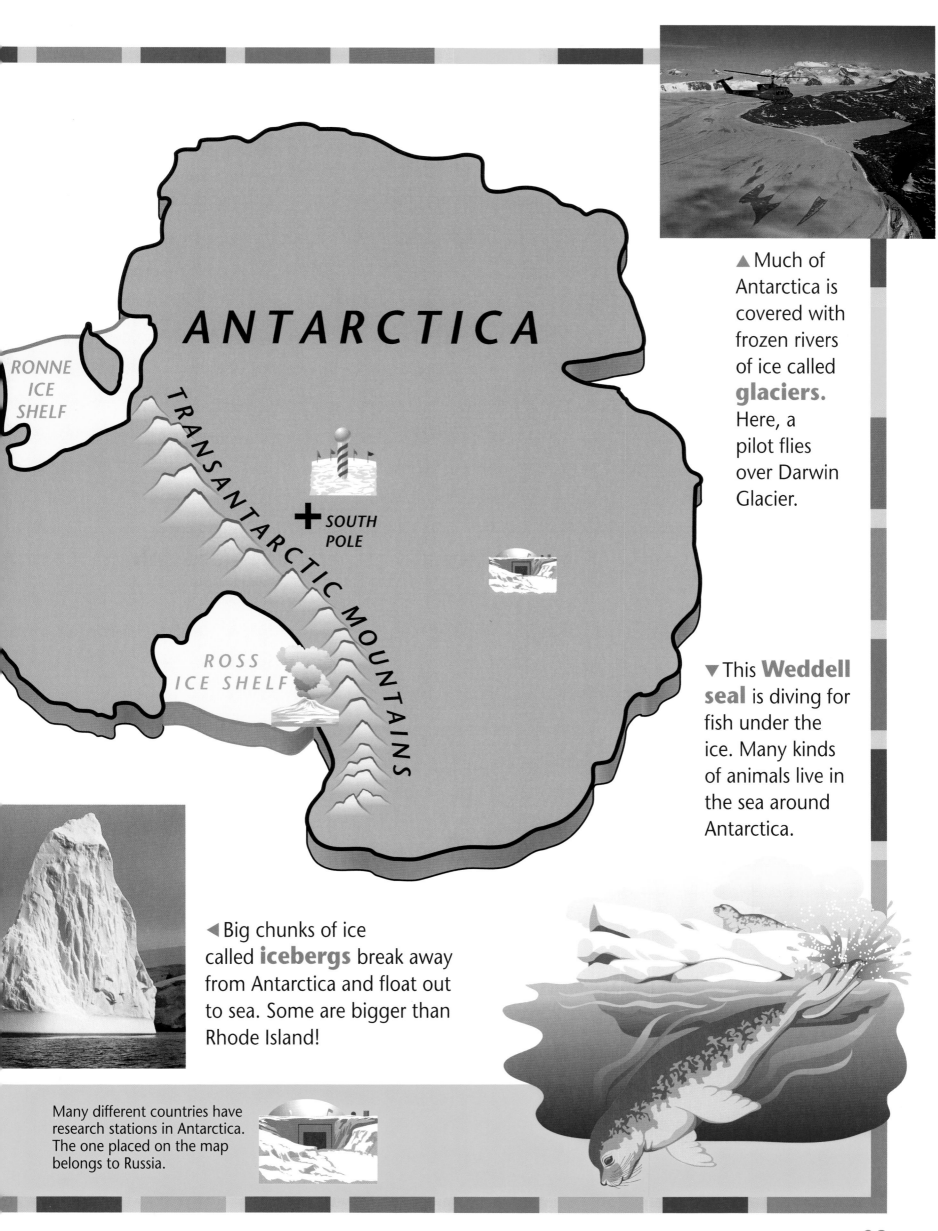

ANTARCTICA

RONNE
ICE
SHELF

TRANSANTARCTIC MOUNTAINS

+ SOUTH
POLE

ROSS
ICE SHELF

▲ Much of Antarctica is covered with frozen rivers of ice called **glaciers.** Here, a pilot flies over Darwin Glacier.

▼ This **Weddell seal** is diving for fish under the ice. Many kinds of animals live in the sea around Antarctica.

◀ Big chunks of ice called **icebergs** break away from Antarctica and float out to sea. Some are bigger than Rhode Island!

Many different countries have research stations in Antarctica. The one placed on the map belongs to Russia.

Family Fun

Young children are natural geographers, eager to explore the world around them. Here are simple activities you can do with your kids to help them get started.

1 **Look for round objects** in your home, such as a ball or an orange. Pick one, then discuss whether it is possible to see more than one side of the object at a time. Mark one side of the object with a dot, then hold up the object with the dotted side turned away. Can you see the dot? Compare the object to a real globe or to the one on page 5. Discuss if it is possible to see the far side of the globe.

If you have a globe at home, look at it together. Find your continent and your country. Then look to see what is on the opposite side of the world. Is it land or water? Name the places you would have to cross to get there. Talk about visiting some of these places.

Guess what I am!

▼I am a man-made structure about 3,000 miles long. I was built to keep out enemies.

What am I? Can you find me in the atlas?

▲I am the world's longest river. These boats use me to carry goods from town to town.

What am I? Can you find me in the atlas?

▼I am the south-ernmost point on the Earth. It is very difficult for people to get to me.

What am I? Can you find me in the atlas?

2 **Open the atlas to the world map** on pages 6–7 and look at it together. What is the blue background? What are the green areas? Now ask your child to close his or her eyes and put a finger anywhere on the map. Then say, "Open your eyes. Did your finger land in the water or on the land?"

Repeat the exercise, moving the book slightly so that your child's finger doesn't always come down in the same spot. Out of five tries, how many times does he or she land on water? On land? Does Earth have more land or more water? Point out that more of the planet is covered by water than by land.

3 **Open the atlas to the U.S. map** on pages 14–15 and, together, locate your home state. Compare it to surrounding states in size, nearness to water, shape, etc. Discuss other states you have visited and locate them. Do relatives live in other states? If so, locate those. In what direction from your state do the relatives live? Ask your child to think who lives farthest from your home state.

Turn to the map on pages 10–11. Figure out where your state is on this map. Do you live in an area of forest, grassland, or desert? Are there mountains in your state? Talk about what it would be like to live where the land is different.

4 **Look at family photographs** with your child. Point out that the people are much smaller in photographs than in real life. Discuss the idea that maps are like photographs in that they shrink all the objects— mountains, rivers, oceans, countries, and so on—that they feature. Suggest that together you create your own landscape in a sandbox or with modeling clay. Use the drawing on pages 8–9 as a guide.

Look down on your scene from above and introduce the concept of a bird's-eye view. Explain that maps are drawn as if seen from above. Now help your child draw a map of the landscape. Add symbols like those on the physical map on pages 10–11.

▲ I shoot lots of hot water and steam high into the air. You can see me if you visit Yellowstone National Park.

What am I? Can you find me in the atlas?

▼ I can climb mountains. My wool is used to make warm blankets.

What am I? Can you find me in the atlas?

▲ I am a huge coral reef, and lots of sea creatures make their homes in me.

What am I? Can you find me in the atlas?

▼ I have tall towers with domes that look like onions. I am in Russia.

What am I? Can you find me in the atlas?

Glossary

canal A canal is a narrow waterway that people have built across the land. The Panama Canal was built across the country of Panama.

capital city A capital city is the place where a country's government is located. Washington, D.C., is the capital city of the United States.

coast A coast is land that borders an ocean.

desert A desert is a place that gets very little rain or snow. It can be sandy or rocky, hot or cold. The Sahara is the world's largest desert.

ice cap An ice cap is a permanent sheet of thick ice that covers land. Greenland and Antarctica both have ice caps.

ice shelf An ice shelf is a thick sheet of ice that sticks out beyond the land into the sea. The largest ice shelves are in Antarctica.

lake A lake is a body of water that is surrounded by land.

mountain A mountain is the highest kind of land. Mount Everest is the highest mountain.

peninsula A peninsula is a piece of land that sticks out into the water. Italy and Florida are examples of peninsulas.

rain forest A rain forest is a woodland that grows in a place that is very wet and usually quite warm. The Amazon rain forest is the largest in the world.

river A river is a large stream of water that flows across the land. The Nile is the world's longest river.

tundra Tundra is a cold region with low plants that grow only during warm months.

volcano A volcano is an opening in the Earth through which melted rock from deep inside the Earth forces its way out onto the surface. Some mountains are volcanoes.

West Indies West Indies is the name for thousands of warm, sunny islands located in the ocean between North America and South America. Cuba is the largest one of these islands.

wetland A wetland is an area of land, such as a swamp or a marsh, that is mostly covered with water. The Everglades is a wetland.

Pronunciation Guide

Note: The accented syllable is in capital letters.

Ayers	ARZ	gondolas	GAHN duh luz
carnaval	kar nah VAL	Himalaya	hih muh LAY uh
Denali	duh NAH lee	Kilimanjaro	kih lih mun JAR o
Erebus	ER uh bus	Masai	MAH sigh
eucalyptus	you kuh LIP tus	Tasmanian	taz MAY nee un
feluccas	fuh LOO kuz		
gauchos	GOW choz		
Ganges	GAN jeez		

National Geographic Society

John M. Fahey, Jr.
President and Chief Executive Officer

Gilbert M. Grosvenor
Chairman of the Board

Nina D. Hoffman
Senior Vice President

William R. Gray
Vice President and Director of the Book Division

Staff for this book

Nancy Laties Feresten
Director of Children's Publishing

Suzanne Patrick Fonda
Project Editor

Marianne R. Koszorus
Art Director of Children's Publishing

Carl Mehler
Director of Maps

Sharon Davis Thorpe
Designer

Susan McGrath
Writer

Marilyn Mofford Gibbons
Illustrations Editor

Thomas L. Gray
Map Editor

Matt Chwastyk
Michelle H. Picard
Gregory Ugiansky
Map Research and Production

Marcia Pires-Harwood
Text and Illustration Research

Jennifer Emmett
Associate Editor

Jo Tunstall
Editorial Assistant

Janet Dustin
Illustrations Assistant

R. Gary Colbert
Production Director

Lewis R. Bassford
Production Manager

Ellen Teguis
Marketing Director, Trade Books

Lawrence M. Porges
Marketing Coordinator

Vincent P. Ryan
Manufacturing Manager

Consultants

Peggy Steele Clay
Teacher-in-Residence National Geographic Society

Billie M. Kapp
Co-coordinator Connecticut Geographic Alliance

Illustrations Credits

Map art by Stuart Armstrong

All other art (unless otherwise indicated) by Barbara Leonard Gibson

Front cover globe digitally created by Slim Films; back cover (upper left), Stone/Lori Adamski-Peek; (art, both), Barbara Leonard Gibson; (bottom left), Marilyn Mofford Gibbons; (bottom right), Daniel J. Cox/Natural Exposures; page 4 Hal Pierce: NASA Goddard Laboratory for Atmospheres, data from NOAA; 5 (globe), Slim Films; 6 (compass art), Theophilus Britt Griswold; 14 (upper), Stone/Lori Adamski-Peek; 14 (lower), Jon Schneeberger; 15 (upper), Mrs. Edi Ann Otto; 15 (lower), Paul Chesley; 16 (upper), Stone/Trevor Wood; 16 (lower), Flip Nicklin; 17, Richard Nowitz; 18, Kenneth Love; 19 (upper), Stone/John Marshall; 19 (lower), Stone/Orion Press; 20 (upper), Sam Abell; 20 (lower), Marilyn Mofford Gibbons; 21, Todd Gipstein; 22, George F. Mobley; 23 (upper), James L. Stanfield; 23 (lower), Daniel J. Cox/Natural Exposures; 24 (upper), Stone/D. E. Cox; 24 (lower), Lu Zhi; 25, Marilyn Mofford Gibbons; 26 (upper), Medford Taylor; 26 (lower), Stone/Lonnie Duka; 26–27, Medford Taylor; 28–29 (all), George F. Mobley.

Acknowledgments

We are grateful for the assistance of Gertrude Burr, Director of the Bethesda Montessori School, for her guidance in the initial planning of this atlas, to NG Image Collection, and to Peggy Candore, Lyle Rosbotham, and Robert W. Witt of the National Geographic Book Division.

ISBN 0-7922-7576-4

Copyright © 2000 National Geographic Society

Published by the National Geographic Society. All rights reserved. Reproduction of the whole or any part of the contents without written permission from the publisher is prohibited.

Printed in Spain

The world's largest nonprofit scientific and educational organization, the National Geographic Society was founded in 1888 "for the increase and diffusion of geographic knowledge." Since then it has supported scientific exploration and spread information to its more than nine million members worldwide.

The National Geographic Society educates and inspires millions every day through magazines, books, television programs, videos, maps and atlases, research grants, the National Geographic Bee, teacher workshops, and innovative classroom materials.

The Society is supported through membership dues and income from the sale of its educational products. Members receive NATIONAL GEOGRAPHIC magazine—the Society's official journal— discounts on Society products, and other benefits.

For more information about the National Geographic Society and its educational programs and publications, please call 1-800-NGS-LINE (647-5463) or write to the following address:

National Geographic Society
1145 17th Street N.W.
Washington, D.C. 20036-4688
U.S.A.

Visit the Society's Web site: www.nationalgeographic.com